the verve

First published in Great Britain in1998 by Chameleon Books

an imprint of André Deutsch Ltd

76 Dean Street

London W1V 5HA

André Deutsch Ltd is a subsidiary of VCI plc

www.vci.co.uk

Design: Neal Townsend for JMP Ltd

Picture research: Karen Tucker for JMP Ltd

1 3 5 7 9 10 8 6 4 2

Printed in and bound by Butler and Tanner, Frome and London

A catalogue record for this book is available from the British Library

ISBN 0 233 99409 2

The only sound to break the Welsh night was the shattering of glass followed by high, manic laughter and sporadic applause. Producer Owen Morris, best known for his work with Oasis, stood unsteadily on the studio mixing desk, gleefully indicating the hole in the glass. The remnants of his vodka and tonic skidded across the wooden floor. The hollow boom exploded in the silence and The Verve's attention was momentarily focused. One pane of expensive studio glass was destroyed. Someone started to giggle as loops of The Verve's A Northern Soul filtered through the speakers. There was a suggestion that they could destroy the studio's £100,000 tape machine to evoke the sound that would give this, their second album, a fitting finish. Things were getting hazy.

I've seen Syd Barrett lying in my sleeping bag in the recording studio.

if I wanna

myself in

for ten

me? It w

. . . if I wanna fucking involve myself in some mindless violence for ten minutes, who's to stop me? It was all paid for

In 1995 The Verve would implode, wash themselves up on a shore of decadence and self-indulgence. The recording session for A Northern Soul would enter rock legend as a collection of lurid stories and gruesome hearsay echoing in stories of drug-fuelled jam sessions that became extensive recording sessions and bouts of reckless violence. The totalled cab fares to and from the local pub alone were, it was said, enough to make grown men shudder. The pane of studio glass wasn't an isolated incident, merely a slender part of a litany of destructiveness and nerve-shredding hedonism that wouldn't have looked out of place in the pages of Kenneth Anger's Hollywood Babylon.

'I was going crazy, man,' Ashcroft later blithely admitted to Q magazine.

'Good crazy, though. If you ain't been that crazy, you're not living. We turned up one day... and the studio guy had locked the control room... He was so fucking frightened of what we were gonna do and I don't blame him... I suppose what I learned from it was how to channel the energy. When I was jumping over cars in some car park in Wales, I could have been in the studio making fucking unbelievable music.'

Unrepentant though he was, Ashcroft admitted it was a very deep hole in to which he'd dug himself. 'I suppose the tail end of that was my lowest point. Lowest point mentally. The psychosis, I've had it all. I've seen visions come out from nowhere, I've seen Syd Barrett lying in my sleeping bag in the recording studio... It frightens the life out of you because once you lose that control over your thought processes to that extent, you're fucked, man. But if you're caning anything, you're gonna get to the point where the demons come and I was seeing the fucking demons.'

Ashcroft wasn't the only one summoning up spirits. Their hefty recording and touring schedule was driving a hole through the middle of the band. The previous summer, they'd toured the US as part of Perry Farrell's rolling, city-to-city Lollapalooza festival. Inter-band relationships were already threatening to crumble. The now familiar excesses were manifesting themselves in the physical realm with drummer Peter Salisbury and a Verve roadie being arrested after trashing a hotel room in Kansas City. Ashcroft, talking again to Q, recalled the carnage with a grin.

'It was just an explosion of some emotion and you had to do something... It's about entering into the cartoon world of Spinal Tap, just for the laugh. But I know where I exist in my head and what level I'm on... But if I wanna fucking involve myself in some mindless violence for ten minutes, who's to stop me? It was all paid for.'

Guitarist Nick McCabe fell into a spiral of depression, while Ashcroft, who now looked deadly earnest in his pursuit of rock and roll infamy, collapsed from dehydration. He blacked out then started to convulse after coming off stage. By the time they got him into an ambulance he'd manage to recover enough to raise a cocky, ironic thumb. It seemed to say, I'm alright, marvellous.

He's since said he found the experience both terrifying and funny, but he believes he almost died.

'I was having fits, the whole business. When I was in the

'When I was jumping a

park in Wales, I could

studio making fucking

er cars in some car

ave been in the

unbelievable music.'

ambulance, I remember putting my thumb up, taking the piss. Funny. But funny and scary 'cause I thought I was gonna die. I had some mad doctor holding me cock while I was trying to pee in a bottle and there were two drips coming out of me arms. You just think, nah, man, I know now I'm really lucky I didn't die.'

But the party wasn't over. On the contrary, it had hardly begun. It was while touring the critically acclaimed A Northern Soul album, that in-fighting, broken by protracted bouts of tense silence, especially between vocalist Richard Ashcroft and guitarist Nick McCabe, started pulling the band to pieces. After a successful and well received appearance, one balmy Sunday in August 1995, at the T In the Park Festival, Ashcroft left the stage and then the band. The internal shockwaves were said to have sent the rest of the band spinning. Ashcroft left for the West Country, muttering that the band couldn't go on like this anymore and then, as he had done countless times in the past, disappeared.

In September, The Verve released the History single. The Face said it was the single of the summer. The sleeve artwork, much like the band, confounded expectations. It showed the band peering gloomily out. Four faces, framed beneath a Times Square cinema awning, bearing the legend, 'All Farewells Should Be Sudden'. But it wasn't quite over yet. Ψ

In 1993 Richard Ashcroft said something he will, in retrospect, never be allowed to forget. History, he said, has a place for us. It may take us three albums, but we will be there. At the beginning of the decade, Richard Ashcroft was known among the music press as Mad Richard. All stuttering pose, a raw-boned libertine fleshed out to resemble, ironically, a dazed Jagger. He spoke of astral travel; of wanting to fly. Hobbies included dropping acid at the local Odeon as Tim Robbins' twisted psychological Vietnam drama Jacob's Ladder played out on the screen. He would tell the NME that taking acid was much more than a simple means to an end. It allowed him to escape from the doldrums of his life. He used it as a tool to get into his music so that he could get something out.

I thought fuck this, can do something positive. can do something great

George Best's maverick approach to the game had influenced the young Ashcroft to the point where he couldn't fit in with a team that was employing a grid-style system of playing

He spoke like someone discovering something very real for the first time.

'If you're experiencing acid, it's the classic thing of your boundaries being taken away so you can see things you never thought you'd see. And you want to relate that to what you're saying. You want to relate to bigger things than chips and Co-ops and Tetley's bitter. You want to relate to suns and flying.

'I'd put travelling and seeing another country on a par with it. Because when it comes down to it, you still wake up the next morning and you're still in Wigan and you're still looking out of the same window at the same view.'

Ashcroft dreamed his dreams quite openly, professing an ambition that, in print, resembled little more than fractious arrogance. His berating of any so-called musical peers became legendary. You felt he either had star quality sealed in his bones or was so entranced by his own message that the true essence of what he, or The Verve, was trying to do or say threatened to be lost.

At his comprehensive school in Wigan, he was known as the Cancer of the Class. His childhood, however, was brought to an abrupt halt at the age of eleven when his father Frank died of a blood clot on the brain. Unsurprisingly, it was a turning point in the young boy's life. As he told Melody Maker, 'I learned early. My father died when I was really young. He'd worked nine to five all his life and he suffered and got nowhere... I immediately realised that this wasn't the life for me... I found out how quickly someone can die, just be wiped out... I thought, fuck this, I can do something positive. I can do something great. I'm gonna make something of myself.'

Instinctively disinclined to accept social norms – the rigours of an eight-hour working day, the entrenchment of class, the patterns of school, work and ultimately death – Ashcroft's internal course had been set. Speaking to The Face, he recalled his father with a genuine fondness, explaining the philosophy that had suddenly been impressed upon him by circumstance.

'... I wouldn't be here now if he hadn't died. God knows what I would be doing. That's the only thing death gives you, isn't it? That one moment of realisation, that makes a mockery of any authority from then on. Because you know from there on that it's all fucking bullshit. None of it makes sense. None of it. You have to go out there and see what happens.'

He would later recall that, while his classmates were playing with Action Men, he was attempting to define the worthwhile aspects of life, to breathe meaning into the fate that had taken his father from him.

Pele and George Best were the pin-ups on his wall and he took to football with a similar vigour that he would later enlist in his pursuit of the rock 'n' roll life. As in music, he had a rogue talent that saw him as a regular for the Upholland Boys team as well as winning him a place at the Bobby Charlton Soccer School. Unfortunately, his love of the Manchester United hero was frowned upon. Best's maverick approach to the game had influenced the young Ashcroft to the point where he couldn't fit in with a team that was employing a grid-style system of playing. Ashcroft wanted to take the ball and run it all over the field. His coach and team-mates did not.

His earnest approach to the game led to a spectacular meeting with future Verve drummer Peter Salisbury on the pitch, when Ashcroft broke his ankle in a tackle that can only be described as both reckless and heartfelt. History recalls that they also had a fist fight on the first day of school. Salisbury, in retrospect, reckoned Ashcroft to be a foot taller than everyone else in the schoolyard and as fully formed then as he is now. The result of the fight is unknown.

Ashcroft's mum was a hairdresser who gave full flight to her son's desire to be different. By the time he was thirteen, Ashcroft

I went from **Adonis**
to scrubbing bogs

n a big high chair

would be spending every Friday night at the salon where his mum worked, experimenting with dyes, styles and bleach. He went from a straw-coloured 'Andy Warhol' (even then it seems his points of reference reached outside of his north of England base), to a purple thatch that he promptly attempted to turn black, resulting in an unfortunate blue. He toyed with an enigmatic quiff with sideburns, a perm, blond streaks and finally a nightmare footballer's affair with a jumble of curls set solely at the back of his head. As he quite proudly pointed out to Vox magazine, 'Yes! I was that lad.'

By the time he was sixteen, he was displaying a disenchantment and world weariness beyond his years. Nothing seemed to make sense to him. One June afternoon he simply stood up and walked out of a religion and philosophy exam. The sun was shining and the day looked both inviting and real. The paperwork set out before him made no sense, not because it was beyond his understanding in an academic sense, it simply didn't stand to reason to stay inside when the real world was just beyond the window. His exit caused a mild alarm that finally built to a frenzy with the school having the canal dredged, thinking Ashcroft had thrown himself into the murky water. It was suggested that he have a chat with the school psychiatrist; he suggested otherwise.

Ashcroft told his careers master that he wanted to be a rock 'n' roll star. Trawl through The Verve cuttings now and it's a familiar proclamation. Journalists have been known to tut and nod at this refrain, though less so since the success of Urban Hymns. His master suggested he take up the role of lifeguard at Wigan Baths instead. On his first day at work it transpired that the eight-stone Richard Ashcroft didn't possess the requisite 25m badge necessary for the person taking on the post of trainee lifeguard. He spent the day cleaning the toilets.

'I went from an Adonis in a big high chair to scrubbing bogs. So I thought: That's enough of this work business – fuck it,' he reasoned to Vox magazine, explaining his early retirement.

Allies, as he would find out again later, are found in the most unlikely places and, after his dad's death, he eventually found solace in the shape of his stepfather, Doug. A former teacher turned biographer, he traced the life story of Alfred Bestall,

verve

All In The Mind

author of the Rupert Bear stories. Ashcroft's compulsive, recalcitrant teenage years were to be equated with a stepdad who encouraged a love of music, who bought the sixteen-year old a motorbike and who taught him about life outside of Wigan and life outside of himself. It was he who first cultivated and then harnessed Ashcroft's interest in astral projection, creative visualisation, chaos theory and astrology.

In an interview with Melody Maker in 1992, the then admittedly wigged-out singer confessed that in years to come he didn't think flight would be beyond man or beyond him. It sounded fanciful, maybe pharmaceutically coloured, but it impressed upon the reader how much his guardian's beliefs had helped to shape him.

'I've got a stepfather who's seriously into meditation and I've heard of him raising the temperature in a room or turning sticks in water just through the forces in his mind. Things like that influenced me so much. I was stuck in Wigan with no job but my mind was hundreds of miles away in the sky and in the sea. It's all escapism, about being somewhere else.' Ψ

'You want to relate to bigger things than chips and Co-ops and Tetley's bitter. You want to relate to suns and flying'

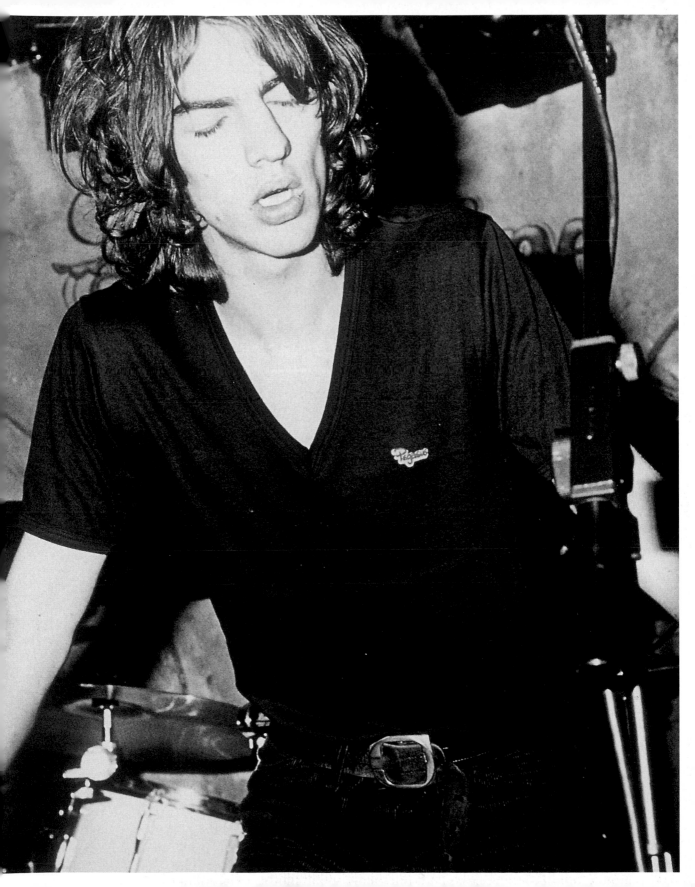

>>**the verve•bitter sweet**<<chapter three

In retrospect, it seemed inevitable that Richard Ashcroft and The Verve should attain some kind of star status. At Upholland Boys, they'd already spent their formative years in and out of bands together, with line-ups that would occasionally include the now fully-fledged member, Simon Tong. In 1990, while still in their teens, they decided to form, as they were then known, Verve. The four piece, with Ashcroft on vocals, Peter Salisbury on drums and Simon Jones on bass, would eventually be completed by a reputed guitar virtuoso from a local college called Nick McCabe. After less than a year of inspired rehearsal and an infusion of head rock, along with some Stones, Led Zeppelin, Sly & The Family Stone, Can, Funkadelic and the Stooges,

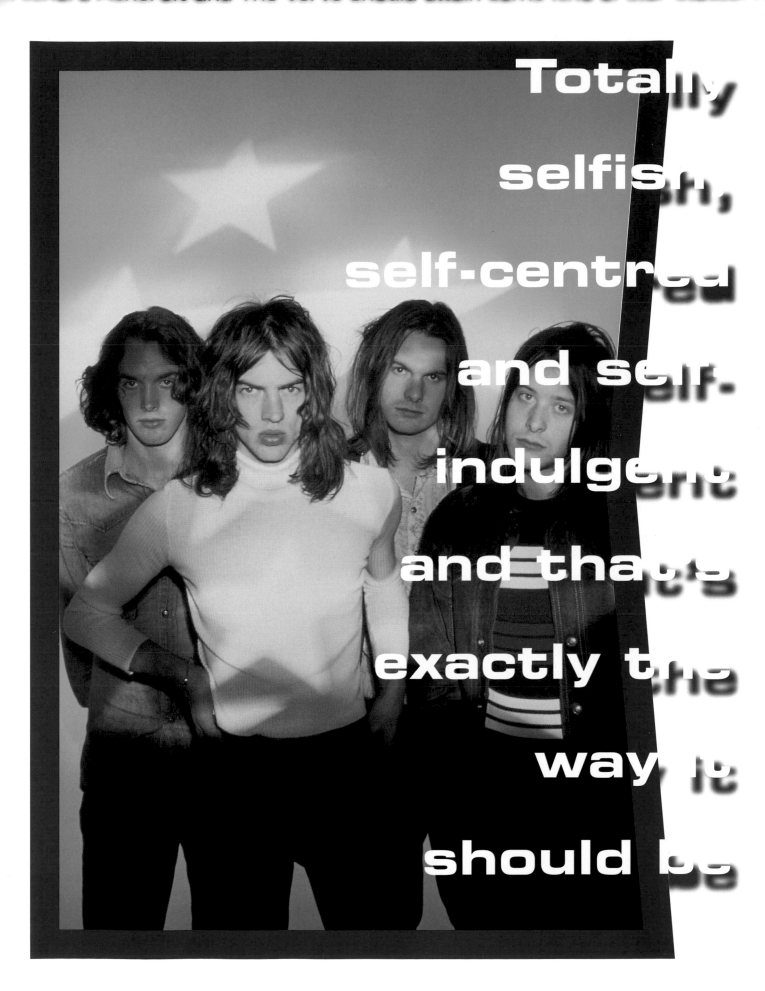

Totally selfish, self-centred and self-indulgent and that's exactly the way it should be

Verve suddenly came complete with a demo that typified their eloquent swell of sound. The initial working of their All In The Mind song sounding both fragile and brilliant. Their early shows at places like the Manchester Boardwalk would often be followed by both audience and band decamping to the outskirts of the city to build bonfires, drop acid and trip out in forest parties. Little wonder that, with their musical pedigree and chemically enhanced background, they should begin by creating musical landscapes that resulted in records drenched in colourful psychedelia and stretched out to eight, nine or ten minutes.

In 1991, with the number of gigs they'd played just reaching double figures, Verve travelled south to the King's Head pub in Fulham to play third on the bill in a room barely a quarter full. The reaction, from record companies, was nothing short of startling. Dave Boyd, now known to the band as Beautiful Davey Boyd, the head of Virgin subsidiary Hut, who eventually signed the band, recalls the near-revelatory moment he first saw the band play live. 'Richard was climbing the monitor rig in front of about twenty people,' he told Q magazine. 'I thought it was absolutely amazing.'

It was their fierce ambivalence to audience reaction, with Ashcroft staring blankly into the crowd, the band suddenly muted then volatile, which was to impress all those who witnessed them on those first trips to London. Producer John Leckie, best known for his work with the Stone Roses and Radiohead and who would eventually produce Verve's debut album, A Storm In Heaven, was equally smitten by their performance. 'I just knew they were special. They're the only band I've ever approached to work with. What really impressed me was the dynamic of how devastatingly loud they could be. At points you could hear a pin drop – and then it would just explode.'

The following year, Verve returned to the work set out on their initial demos and released the All In The Mind single, backed with the loquacious A Man Called Sun. Their first attempt at recording what was to be their debut single was

There's nothing like the elation of seeing someone stood static at the beginning, icy cold, a complete virgin to your music and then to see them being completely overpowered and engrossed by it. That transition is what it's all about only slightly marred by the fact that their initial attempt to put anything down on tape was made while the band members were strung out on hallucinogenics. The session was halted until everyone had come down so that they could start again. The press reaction to their sublime, groove-based freak-outs, combined with Ashcroft's outpourings – concerning himself with higher thinking on one hand and then trashing his musical peers on the other – was one of mild alarm and finger-pointing.

Ashcroft's bullish self-belief and supreme confidence were evident in an early interview with the now defunct Indiecator magazine.

'We could easily make a three-minute classic hit. Everybody knows the ingredients, but what's the point of doing something for ten years of your life, something you have always dreamed about, just to wake up one day and realise that you have been a fake?'

Thus, Richard became Mad Richard to the critics, some of whom considered their early work quiet genius set outside the early '90s indie guitar boom, whereas others considered them nothing more than a bunch of nutters from Wigan who should probably go back there sooner rather than later. The band's attitude did little to help matters.

In interview situations they were in turn vocal then taciturn. In 1992, guitarist Nick McCabe told Melody Maker that the band were 'Totally selfish, self-centred and self-indulgent and that's exactly the way it should be.' Ashcroft would give credence to those sentiments. Simply put, this was their thing, no one else's. 'I don't want us to be an indie band in the indie chart... I want us to be a world band in the world chart. We don't want to fit in. I don't want kids to buy our records and think they could do it. I want them to think... it's so special. It's unique. Great bands have only ever formed to satisfy themselves. We do this for ourselves, always have done. And as long as I'm satisfied, we'll progress, do better gigs, make better records.' There was little by way of apology. They rounded indignantly on their record company and threatened to

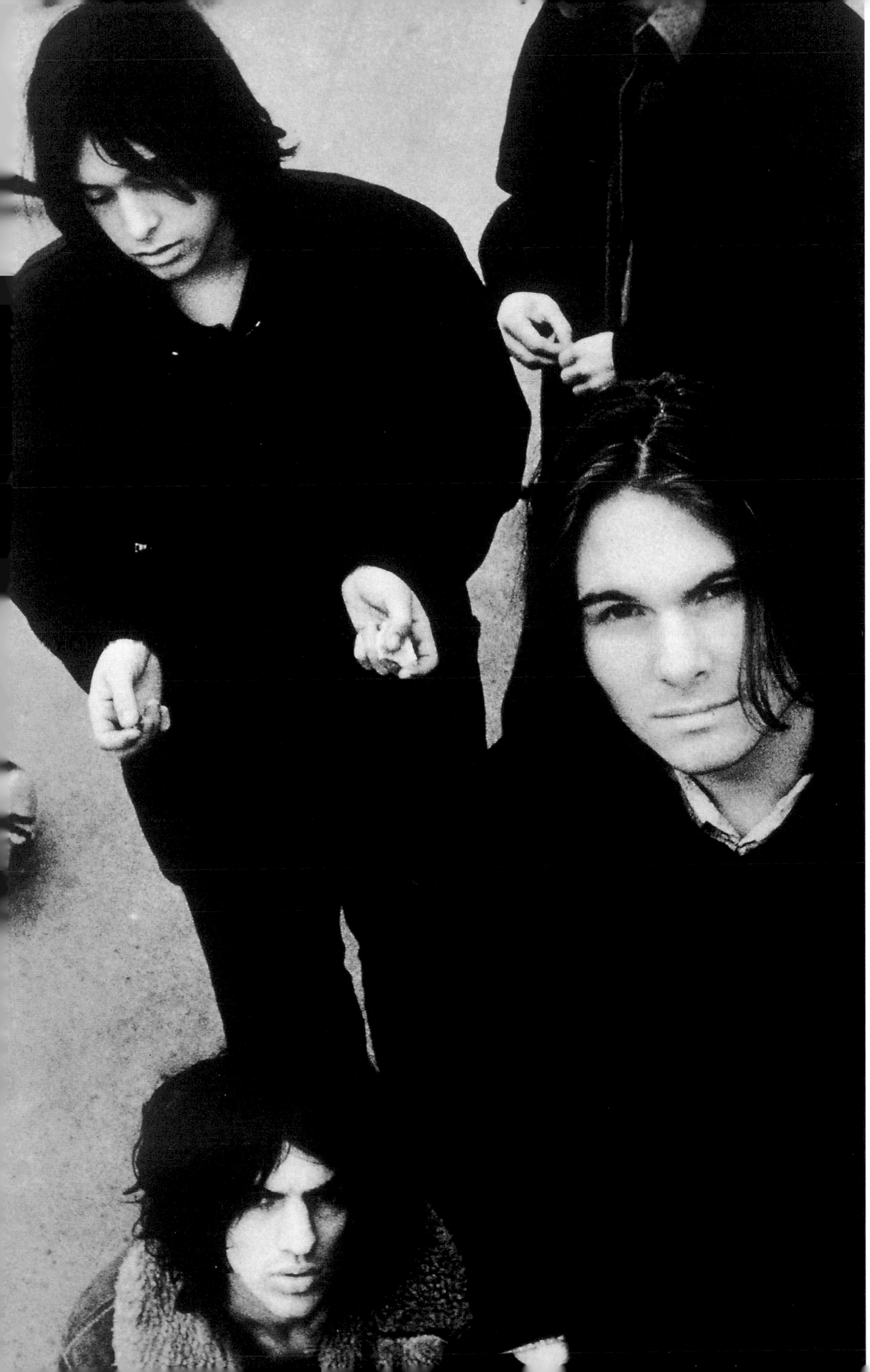

>>**the verve•bitter sweet**<<already there

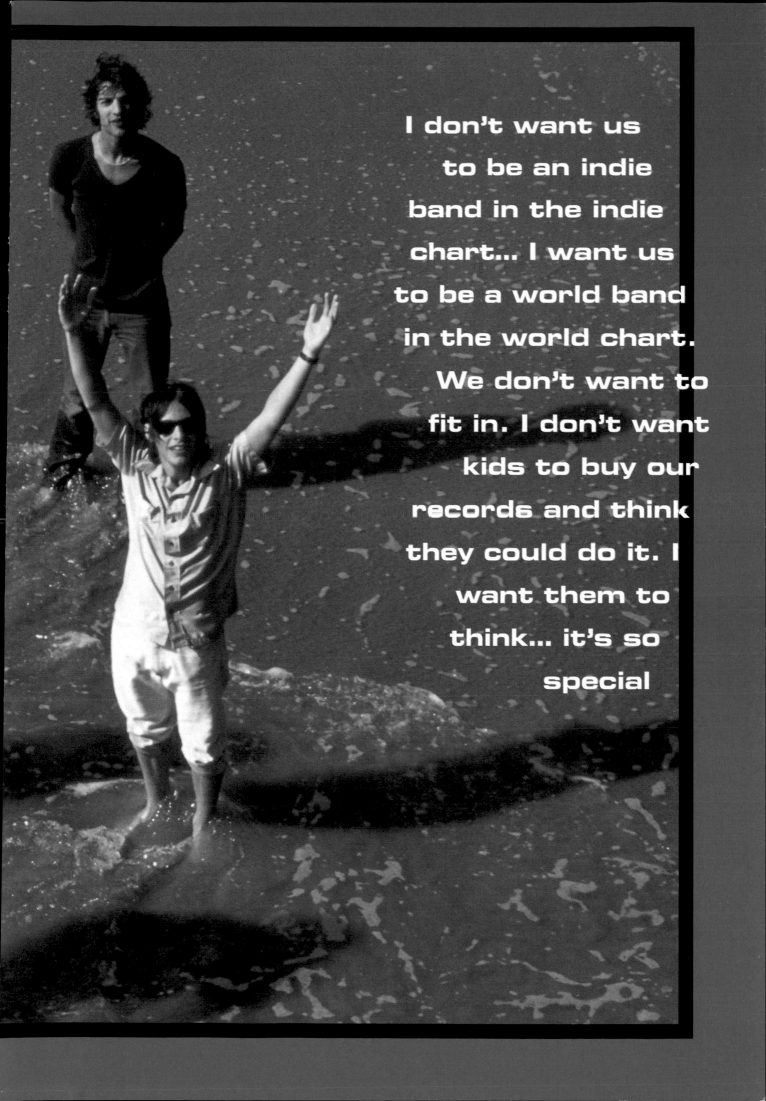

I don't want us to be an indie band in the indie chart... I want us to be a world band in the world chart. We don't want to fit in. I don't want kids to buy our records and think they could do it. I want them to think... it's so special

It touched me.
It's about
someone
who's got
strength but
who's fragile
as fuck as well

**It touched me.
It's about
someone
who's got
strength but
who's fragile
as fuck as well**

on Noel Gallagher's

Cast No Shadow

break up if the people in suits didn't back off. They were a jumble of contradictions, but always utterly insistent that they were the future, that the best was yet to come.

Their second single, She's A Superstar, came in at a little under nine minutes. The b-side, (Wanna Know Wanna Be Wanna) Feel, possibly in an effort not to be outdone, was nearer eleven. It was rumoured that the length of the songs was simply to agitate their record company. Listening to those songs now, the rolling disquiet, set in the wash of sounds, becomes almost orchestral. It probably does help if you've dropped a load of gear, though.

By the time the third single, Gravity Grave, was released, the press had caught up with the music, though patently still could not come to grips with Ashcroft himself. The listening public, however, were hardly inflamed. The singles all did well in the independent charts but in terms of real sales the reaction was distinctly muted.

The band managed to cause more disquiet by not actually putting the first three singles on their debut album. It was with the release of the Blue single, in 1993, that somehow managed to be intangible yet ludicrously close to magnificent, that hints appeared suggesting Verve had the grace to fortify Ashcroft's dramatic boasts.

A Storm In Heaven followed that summer. Recorded with John Leckie at the Sawmills studio in Cornwall, it paraded an ambitious sweep of psychedelia, but promised something approaching a point of focus with songs like the aforementioned Blue and the album opener, Star Sail.

They told Indiecator, 'We smoke a lot, but the music comes first. Well, maybe it doesn't come first all of the time.' The band's passions and beliefs were blended with an incense-tinged ambience and gentle rhythms that were as intoxicating as the heavy smoke in which they shrouded themselves. Like much of the praise that had been heaped upon their live performances, on record they proved they could still be both dramatic and calm.

The album cover featured a Verve logo aflame inside Thor's Cave in Staffordshire. A lone, bleached-out figure

stands in the entrance, arms reaching upwards to some higher plane. The band appear in a gloomy black and white portrait staring defiantly out from the sleeve, toy dolls perched either side of them. A car with a VERVE number plate burns brightly on the back cover. The band sit close by, indifferent to the carnage, either reading papers or considering a chess game. Their message wasn't instantly clear.

The recording also heightened the debate over whether Ashcroft was certifiable, or simply operating on his own indiscernible wavelength. Stories abound of the singer appearing at the studio with no shoes or change of clothes. One night, he and Peter Salisbury took out a couple of canoes, some spliff and a bottle of whisky to explore a local river estuary. By ten that evening studio staff were about to phone the coastguard, as the sea was a mere half a mile away and both canoeists had neglected to pick up lifejackets, when the pair sauntered back in to the studio amazed by all the fuss.

Former manager and publicist John Best says he remembers the times that Ashcroft had stayed with him. He recalls, with some fondness, the fact that most of his underwear would disappear after the singer had spent any length of time at his house. Also, Ashcroft managed to mislay his passport so many times that the authorities suggested that perhaps he was selling them on at a reasonable profit. For his part, Ashcroft tends to focus on the barefoot, lost weekend-type of moments the most.

'I remember coming down, walking around looking for our press officer, in bare feet, like an absolute maniac, with me hair down to me shoulders, fucking off me head,' he relates to Vox. 'I'm still the same person, obviously, but I'm not as "Waaaah!" about it all.'

There's another Richard Ashcroft story that when he first earned anything like real money, he spent it on having lasagne delivered to his front door every day for five months until the money ran out. He said he did it because it was a rock 'n' roll cliché, though he failed to make clear exactly which one.

There were plenty more to be indulged in, however, like the time when Verve bravely toured with the Black Crowes in 1992. The Crowes taught Ashcroft to slip off his shoes and perform live sets on a Persian rug. Elsewhere, stories of hotel

The Black Crowes taught Ashcroft to slip off his shoes and perform live sets on a Persian rug

trashing and over-indulgence began to circulate around the increasingly confident band with troubling regularity.

On stage, however, Verve were converting audiences who were patently unclear about who the support act were, or exactly what it was they were trying to achieve. Speaking to the NME in the same year, Ashcroft seemed delighted to be able to either turn any preconceived notions over or simply stun the uninitiated.

'There's nothing like the elation of seeing someone stood static at the beginning, icy cold, a complete virgin to your music and then to see them being completely overpowered and engrossed by it. That transition is what it's all about.'

The press, meanwhile, became more intrigued with Ashcroft's antics than anything that the debut album might have to say. Though critically acclaimed, it was his allusions to philosophy and the idea of metaphysical flight that cast a shadow over anything the music might have to offer. As an irate Ashcroft was later to tell Vox, 'We've been ridiculed, we've been too much for people to either describe or understand. The "Mad Richard" thing, that was really orchestrated to divert things. It was very demeaning. And we knew we were one of the most important bands in the world when we started. Everyone can have their opinion, but when it becomes personal towards me, when it doesn't even try and explain what the fucking music sounds like, that used to piss us off big time... People

thought that we were hyped, but for a long time nobody
helped us fuckin' once.'

A Storm In Heaven was to reach a respectable 27 in the UK
charts. Ashcroft considered it a decent enough beginning, but
maintained that the journey would be a long one. The single
Slide Away hinted that there was more to Verve than moody
ramblings and the inability to bring a song in at under six
minutes. Ashcroft knew who his peers were, or at least who
they should be. He talked of leaving the world a legacy of
work that would equate to legendary names of the 1960s, or
the body of work that The Smiths draped all over the 1980s.
He dismissed references to My Bloody Valentine or The Byrds,
while claiming not to be familiar with the dozens of other
bands with whom people were comparing Verve.

As he told Indiecator, he was looking to the future. 'This
album is a big step, but there are a thousand million more to go.'
He wasn't about to take the journey alone, however. He'd
find a musical peer, partner, friend and, perhaps more
importantly, someone who understood, sooner than he thought.

It was while preparing for a club tour to back the 1993 A
Storm In Heaven album that Verve were handed a four-track
demo that featured both Live Forever and Columbia. Quietly
impressed, which was something of shock considering
Ashcroft's barely suppressed disdain for any other
contemporary band who came into view, they offered Oasis
the support slot for all the dates on the tour.

Ashcroft claims the bands became friends instantly. When
he talks about their initial tour together it is with a genuine
warmth and fondness.

'When they were doing Live Forever, there was two
people sat on the floor and there was me on the balcony with
my arms aloft.' He told Q magazine. 'Real moments. Real
fucking moments. And that's why whatever happens, I'll
know them and they'll know me forever because it was
beyond bullshit, before fame, before money, before anything.'
After a power cut at their show in Glasgow, Ashcroft,
Noel Gallagher and Nick McCabe delivered an impromptu
a cappella version of She'll Be Coming Round The Mountain,

with Bonehead on the spoons.

After the Hultsfred Pop Festival in Sweden, at which both bands appeared, a hotel was trashed and the bands were forcibly ejected from the premises and very nearly from the country. To complete the evening, Noel and Ashcroft were eventually tracked down in the early hours of the morning attempting to break into a church in order to get at the communion wine. They only decided to draw the line when it came down to arguing about the merits of Manchester City versus United as, they both agreed, it would only end in violence.

Noel Gallagher found Ashcroft so irresistible as to be moved enough to write Cast No Shadow, from (What's The Story) Morning Glory? about him

Memories, it's said, are made of this.

The friendship was to spill over into their songwriting. Oasis creating their own Slide Away, with a title borrowed from A Storm In Heaven. Stylistically, the Gallaghers were all front and swagger – lyrically manifest with titles like Live Forever, Supersonic and Rock 'n' Roll Star. Ashcroft sang songs called Butterfly and Beautiful Mind, somehow he seemed both fragile and insistent.

Ashcroft attempted to measure their different approaches to music to Vox. 'Maybe our message is a bit more confused. I've always been a big dreamer too, but I get obsessed with the darker side... the soundscapes we create push a definite part of me out. Y'know what? I just think Noel's not got the time. Not got the fucking time, d'you know what I mean? And maybe I think too much.'

That Verve would one day break up, albeit temporarily, seems in retrospect a certainty. Ashcroft wanted musical nirvana, which he openly admitted was near-impossible to achieve. Yet he attempted to reach it while blunting his sensibilities with a diet of drugs and alcohol. His doors of

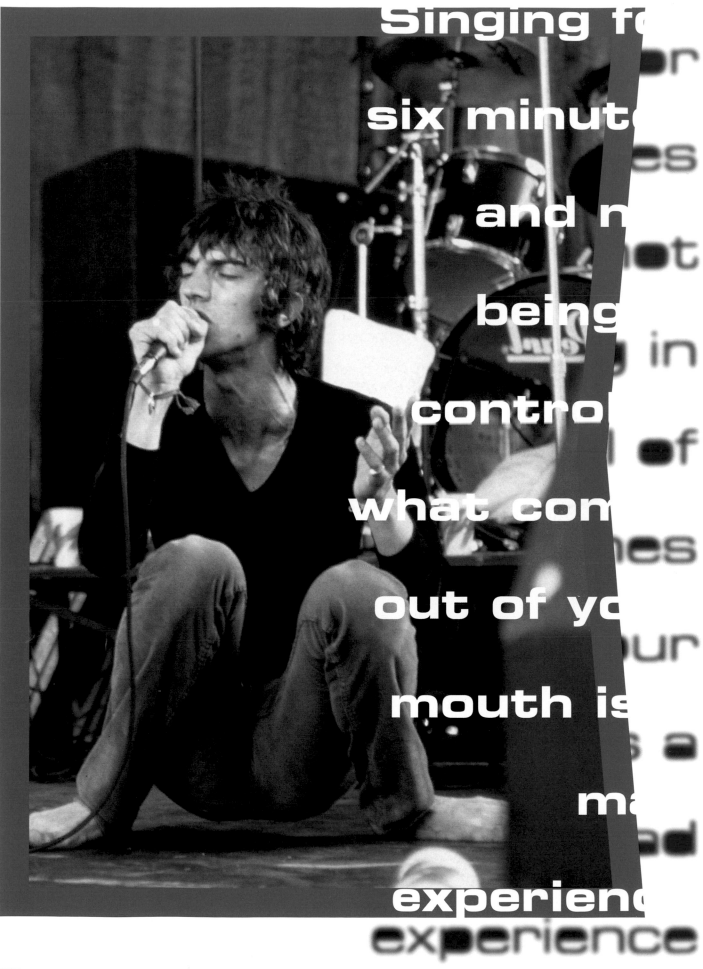

Singing fo
six minut
es
and n
ot
being
g in
contro
l of
what com
es
out of yo
ur
mouth is
s a
ma
ad
experienc
experience

As he told The Face, '... (It was) my dad's rings. Watches. All my records, all my clothes. Everything. Since then I've just had a bag. I've not even caught up. When you've bought the same record or book for the third time, all those Vanilla Fudges and HP Lovecrafts, it gets a bit depressing, you know? But at the end of the day I owed the geezer three grand. I hope his son had a good laugh with it. Sometimes it's good to lose everything.'

He spent the next few months living on the periphery of society, dodging train fares by travelling in the toilet, making and taking money wherever he could; elusive when he was meant to be talking to the press. He was sighted all over the country, but rarely ever really seen. Finally, he moved to London with a solitary plastic bag, slept on a friend's floor and waited for the world to begin to right itself, for the insanity to subside. Much later, as he reassessed the madness and turmoil he'd become immersed in, as a lost weekend had spread in to days and months, he'd tell Vox magazine, 'I just wanted to get back in touch with life again.'

He sounded neither appalled by his actions nor relieved that his transient lifestyle was over. It just sounded like it was time to do something else.

A Northern Soul was released in July 1995 and in the few days that were to follow before the band declared their split, the response to the record had been one of surprise and praise. Within a month of its release it had sold more copies than A Storm In Heaven had managed in two years. The future actually looked set. They had been offered the support slot on the autumn Oasis tours in both the UK and the US. As well as the promise of their own headline shows throughout Europe and Japan.

Their inability to be swayed by promises of success was laudable, but their conviction and dismissal of more conventional routes to stardom were to blight the launch of what happened to be a very good record. In the light of Urban Hymns, it looks unlikely that A Northern Soul will ever receive the rich praise it deserves.

Where their debut album had been filled with spirals of colour and songs muted and washed with a dazzle of ideas left to run wildly out of control, A Northern Soul was more plaintive in its approach. Considering the upheaval that had

One character going through twelve different experiences of pain, elation, sex, loss, romance... all the emotions piled into one album. This is to the point, to the heart and to the soul

Richard Ashcroft on A Northern Soul

Trouble at
the moment
is you've got
all these
Camden
bands who are
just making
instant music,
sliced bread
music. And in
the end that
sort of stuff
just gives you
malnutrition.
It's time for a
cure

that sort of stuff just giv

that sort of stuff ju

...s you malnutritio

gives you **malnutrit**

taken place during the recording at the aptly named Loco
Studios in South Wales with producer Owen Morris, the results
were nothing short of heroic. Twelve heady, soulful tracks that
wouldn't have looked amiss on some Led Zeppelin compilation.
Ashcroft had the concept laid clearly out in his head.

'One character going through twelve different experiences of
pain, elation, sex, loss, romance... all the emotions piled into one
album. This is to the point, to the heart and to the soul.'

A somewhat emotional Morris was said to have trashed speakers,
chairs and windows during the recording. Because, as Ashcroft
pointed out to Vox, 'He was enjoying the song so much.'

Initially, things hadn't seemed so bad. Nick McCabe remembered
the first three weeks in the studio as 'The best three weeks of my life,
because we were just enjoying making music and not thinking about
it,' he told Vox. 'And then it all went nuts. Richard and Owen were
shouting and smashing things up and I was retreating into myself. At
the end it was horrible.'

As Ashcroft remarked dryly, 'If we recorded every album like this
one, we'd be dead.'

Bassist Simon Jones ended up laying most of the blame at producer
Owen Morris's feet. 'Owen was the catalyst, he's as mad as you like...
and we don't need any encouraging. It was all... too much.'

The Gallagher brothers hung out at the studio during recording,
Liam contributing handclaps to History. While a suitably impressed
Noel, on first hearing what was to be their final single for two
years, was heard to remark, 'Fuck me! The bastards!'

The three singles, History, This Is Music and On Your Own,
highlight the strength of songwriting that had somehow been
found while the band were alleged to have been at their most
hedonistic. On Your Own was remarkable in that it was the first
song that Ashcroft had written alone on his acoustic guitar.
The wistful refrain of, 'You come in on your own/And you
leave on your own', embraces the gentle unscrolling of the
song. Beyond the landscapes of psychedelia and mammoth
instrumental interplay that featured so heavily in their earlier
work, there was now a clearer, more dramatic and honest
foundation to their work.

'The first album was wrapped up in imagery and was very

escapist, whereas this one is more personal and more real,' Ashcroft explained to Vox, obviously relishing the profundity and strength of his own songwriting. The results seems to have surprised him more than anyone.

'On Your Own means a lot to me, because it was the first time that I'd really sat down and gone through the process of songwriting – nearly everything else has been written in a jam with the four of us together in a room. Lyrically, I think it's one of the strongest songs to date... '

The success of this new songwriting process had also spilt over into a new song he was just finishing working on at the time. He said it was going to be called The Drugs Don't Work. But the world would have to wait two years to hear that one.

For now he had redefined the band's output, by redefining himself. He was clear-minded about opening himself up for scrutiny. Personal introspection and wondering at the complexities of life and love were part of the new songwriting equation. If he had been running away through the use of vividly detailed musical workouts before, it seemed that now he was completing a full circle; coming back to face himself.

'With this album I felt that I'd discovered something new about myself,' was his response to the album's humanity, when he spoke to Dazed & Confused. 'I'd opened a personal Pandora's box. Things like that just come to you in life. They've probably been there all the time, it's just a question of you actually realising that they're there. And the result has come out in the music. The grooves, the lyrics, the guitar work, they've all joined together to become something extra. The record just sounds like modern rock 'n' roll music.'

The remarkable History was said to have been recorded in one take. Whether this was before or after the systematic destruction of the studio is unclear. But what does remain is that, whereas someone like Noel Gallagher had looked to Ashcroft as inspiration for his lyrics, Ashcroft

The band just couldn't exist any longer. I knew I needed to do it. It would've killed us, it really would've killed us. It wasn't a Nick thing, it was all of us just needing to fuck off

> ## Groups have got an amazing power... It's not the ultimate power or anything, but something just happens when music is really good, and that's the force that keeps us together

had always been looking beyond the simpler avenues of expression and stimulus.

'You know those sailors in myths and legends who would strap themselves to the mast in a storm, just to see what it was like? That's us. Just out there, fucking finding out how it feels.'

History had originally been recorded in demo form at home, using his mother's old Spanish guitar and passages from William Blake's poem, London. Ashford's intention was to utilise part of Blake's work. But, as he told Vox, something else happened instead.

'When I opened my mouth something else poured out. Singing for six minutes and not being in control of what comes out of your mouth is a mad experience. I was tapping into a place where I believe all the great songwriters go, and on every song that I've written on an acoustic guitar since... I've been trying to get back to that place.'

Music Week made it album of the week. While Melody Maker made This Is Music single of the week, suggesting that Verve had updated The Stooges and somehow brought the sound of Detroit to Wigan. The NME saluted what was supposed to be their final single by showering them in plaudits. Applauding their do-it-for-the-music or die attitude. It looked as though the world couldn't possibly get by without The Verve.

After their positive reception in the US on the Lollapalooza tour, and the new album peaking at thirteen in the national charts, The Verve should have been satisfied by their success in the face of almost overwhelming adversity. Who else could have come through the sheer dementia that had passed for a recording session in Wales and remained creatively fecund? Yet how much was sheer facade? What was lurking under the serenity of the four meditative faces staring bleakly out from the cover of A Northern Soul?

On the promotional circuit, in England at least, Ashcroft was still making optimistic noises about the band. Still expressive and upbeat about the power and soul to be found in his band's music, it wasn't the voice of a quitter,

History had originally been recorded as a

demo at home, using his mother's old

Spanish guitar and passages from William

Blake's poem, *London*. Ashford's intention

was to utilise part of Blake's work. But

something else happened instead.

or someone crushed by the weight of excess. From the outside it looked as though The Verve had been through the worst of it and managed to step out the other side intact. He was heard, much like the old Ashcroft, to praise the potency of music, that his position was an enviable one.

'Groups have got an amazing power... and they should make the most of them. It's not the ultimate power or anything, but something just happens when music is really good, and that's the force that keeps us together,' he told Dazed & Confused magazine.

He spoke of feeling optimistic, that having Oasis along on the journey made it an easier one. In the accompanying photo spread he stood barefoot, peering quizzically at the camera, his eyes glazed, like unclear windows. Frankly, he didn't look like he was ever coming down.

The press talked of the band as space cadets. Ashcroft pitted Wigan against the rest of the world when he spoke. He talked of the Northern Soul Circuit, of its followers and speed casualties. The album, he said, was some kind of nod to them. To the ones caught in the long distant afterglow, now playing dominoes in the corner of pubs in his home town.

He slated the south. The whole scene and the way that magazines only really came to focus on what was on their own doorstep He thought the distance between The Verve and London was a good thing. That the miles had let the band grow up musically, intellectually and philosophically. As he was only too happy to point out to Dazed & Confused, things were wrong and The Verve were the ones quite capable of putting it right.

'They're creating monsters down there. There's no soul to it... It stinks. I don't want anything to do with it. They want me to be a media celebrity rather than be someone who plays music... We don't want to be part of anyone else's gang. If people want to join us, then, yeah, great, but we're not looking up to anyone else.

'Music is a soundtrack to my life and my emotions. It has the power to change the way I see the day... Trouble at

> **I remember sitting in a hotel room overlooking the cliffs in Cornwall and Radio One came on and it said, 'The Verve are history and this is their final single, History.' I was more choked than I've ever been in my life**
>
> *Nick McCabe*

the moment is you've got all these Camden bands who are just making instant music, sliced bread music. And in the end that sort of stuff just gives you malnutrition. It's time for a cure.'

With A Northern Soul, full of heart and glorious intention, The Verve seemed capable of feeding the masses. Nick McCabe's guitar work, considering that he admitted the album sessions had driven him into a dark hole inside himself, is nothing less than spectacular. It comes as no surprise that the sessions they were later to put together without the guitarist would be considered unfinished. His dizzying range of sounds pinpointed the peaks and troughs in the songs.

On the final song of the album, the blistering (Reprise), his sense of attack becomes disquieting. Enveloping the song within, turning the language of its discourse upside down before tearing holes along the body of the music. To say it makes your eyes pop open with surprise would be to understate the matter entirely.

Combine this with Ashcroft's new found ability to turn the lyrical spotlight on himself and you had an album that, due to the fact that the band imploded before they could show the world just how lustrous their record might be, would fall through the net.

The spellbinding History illustrated this new approach, built as it was on a garland of strings and with a story that could have been lifted straight from the pages of an open diary, while the tumbling Life's An Ocean was evocative and startling.

The rear sleeve artwork had bassist Simon Jones's face reflected in the chrome facade of the Feelings machine, about to insert his 50c in the coin slot. A neat row of red levers set beneath black and white shots of faces emoting what looked to be sorrow, anguish or anger. It looked like something The Who might have once considered as part of their conceptual artwork. The Verve were to use the machine again later as part of the set for their The Drugs Don't Work video shoot. But that would be when everything had been fixed for good. Before then they'd have to break it all down to build it again.

That was
mad, really;
it just
showed me
that I'm not
a solo
artist. I felt
so alone up
there

When The Verve talk about the break-up now, it all sits shrouded in half-truths, unspoken words and gestures. They draw in on themselves like a fist and the reality can't seem to quite get through the fingers. Even the once vocal Ashcroft retreats into allusion and dismissive waves of his hand.

In recent interviews, the emphasis has been on looking to the future. Blame has been apportioned, but the bones of the matter remain covered over. The Face reported that the band had fired Nick McCabe when he was suffering from what was probably clinical depression — a claim which reportedly infuriated the guitarist to the point where he could barely speak.

Ashcroft, speaking to Q, dismissed the idea that had been circulating, that the meltdown had occurred quite deliberately to shift guitarist Nick McCabe from the axis of the band. 'The band split up because we did have internal problems, yeah, but we all individually had our problems and we'd been through the insane tours, the insane albums, blah blah blah. The band just couldn't exist any longer. I knew I needed to do it. It would've killed us, it really would've killed us. It wasn't a Nick thing, it was all of us just needing to fuck off.'

The band members themselves support this claim, to a point. McCabe eventually exorcised his demons by admitting to bouts of depression and mental illness. It's clear that the band felt the break keenly. Ashcroft admitted to being near tears when the dust had finally settled and he'd realised the impact that ending the band had brought to his life.

'I remember sitting in a hotel room overlooking the cliffs in Cornwall and Radio One came on and it said, "The Verve are history and this is their final single, History". I was more choked than I've ever been in my life,' he confessed to Dazed & Confused. Attempting to explain the comedown, but still unwilling to reveal the full story, he continued, 'I'm The Verve's biggest fan, y'know... the point is, we had to split. I couldn't lie anymore. I don't like living a lie and we had to do it. When we were recording A Northern Soul we went into a scary zone, to places where it takes a long time to come to terms with what went on... Not just drugs... there are things that have gone on in The Verve that I won't be talking about... until the day I die.

> There are things that have gone on in The Verve that I won't be talking about... until the day I die
>
> Nick McCabe

'If we were an American band I might talk about them and go on to sell 15 million albums on the back of it, but because we're from Wigan and we all love each other, we're not gonna start talking about it... Let's just say there was a cloud over us.'

The other members of the band are similarly reticent. Drummer Peter Salisbury's comments on the crash – that it had all become too much – echoed the band's sentiments entirely. McCabe has now taken his departure from the band pretty much on himself.

In interviews he talked of losing the plot, of getting in the way of what the band were doing, especially during the second album sessions, and of letting his personal life bleed all over the body of the band.

In an interview with the NME, McCabe's openness with regard to his earlier problems were as disarming as they were brutal. 'I was really ruining it for everybody in the last year of it... I fucked it up, really... It was me on my own. I have mental problems!

'I have my bad days, but generally everything's worked out for the better... I know what I need to do to make myself happy... It's getting better and better... I've benefited most out of this, really, 'cos I've got a sense of whatever goes wrong doesn't really matter, 'cos I fell to the bottom and it wasn't so bad.'

He also admitted that at some points it had all been too many drugs and not enough communication. But he also added that the answer wasn't in drug psychosis; that the real answer was as mundane as the constant questions about it all. Perhaps the truth lay in something he said to Vox: 'Me and Richard don't always get on, we're polar opposites.'

Whatever lay beneath the rubble of their collapse looks set to stay there. Ashcroft walked and the press spoke of a split that was as inevitable as it was tragic.

The official reason for the rift was given in a press statement by John Best, then the band's manager. It alluded to irreconcilable differences, to art over commerce, to, in a very Verve way, the vibe not being right.

The grooves, the lyrics, the guitar work, they've all joined together to become something extra. The record just sounds like modern rock 'n' roll music

'It is known that Richard had returned from their recent tour feeling strangely underwhelmed by the rapturous reception the band had received,' the statement read. 'And it is also believed that the famously fever pitch of recording of A Northern Soul had taken its toll.'

It also came to light, during an interview that John Best had given Melody Maker, that Ashcroft had temporarily left Loco Studios, and the band, for five days during the recording of the ill-fated second album.

'Richard left for a while during the recording of the album... It was an emotionally fraught time for the band. I admire Richard's integrity, because it's come at a time when everyone had decided that they are a great band... They're not like other bands. They're not doing it to be famous, they're doing it because they're musicians...

'Things change. They were four lads based in Wigan and now they're spread out all over the UK. The expansion that it originally brought wasn't there any more. They wanted to keep meaning it.'

For a band who didn't believe in detractors, the critical acclaim was something they probably expected, the promise of commercial success, which was being felt ever more keenly with the steady sales of A Northern Soul, didn't mean a thing.

Best, speaking later to NME, rang the death knell for the band, citing the break up as very much the decision of the disheartened frontman.

'There won't be a band called The Verve any more and they won't be working together again. But although he (Ashcroft) wasn't happy and had obviously been thinking about this, he's happy now... he's only 23 and he'll do something amazing again.'

The message was clear, there had been two glorious, fractured albums, some remarkable live shows, at once sublime and then shoddy and then an irrecoverable meltdown that seemed to have gone to the heart of the band.

But within weeks at least three of The Verve were back in a studio, with a set of mastertapes marked simply, 'Richard

Ashcroft'. Simon Jones, Peter Salisbury and Ashcroft started working together again, finally calling up old school friend and guitarist Simon Tong, who had initially taught Jones to play guitar, to boost the sound. Nick McCabe went back to Wigan and his daughter, Ellie.

The break-up of the band and what seemed a sudden regrouping of them without him, saddened and shocked the guitarist, as he told The Face: 'It did eat me up a bit... especially when they got Simon in, but then I got so burnt up that I just decided to forget about them. I thought it was all over. It was like my family had collapsed, but I was big enough to cope with it now.'

The band, as was, began work on what would become around fifty songs in varying states of completion. Though, as time was spent in the studio with producers John Leckie and Owen Morris respectively, it became clear to all concerned that without McCabe, or a guitarist of his calibre, the synergy created on their previous albums would be lost.

Ashcroft approached former Stone Roses guitarist John Squire at a party that was being thrown for comedian Eddie Izzard, inviting him to at least play guitar with the singer. Ironically, at the time, it was rumoured that McCabe had been approached about becoming the new guitarist in the Stone Roses. Squire, who was in the throes of putting the Seahorses together, declined the offer. Ashcroft, at the suggestion of his management and bassist Simon Jones, then approached former Suede guitarist Bernard Butler. Rehearsals, which began at Bernard's house and were rumoured to be going splendidly, peaked at around a week. Butler and Ashcroft both agreed that there was very little by way of a spark. The search, it's reasonable to assume, was still on.

As producer John Leckie reasoned to Q, after he'd helped demo up some new material with the band at the end of 1995, the space left by the troubled McCabe was becoming more and more difficult to fill.

'The stuff without Nick sounded good, but it was in desperate need of an instrumentalist, a lead guitarist. You had... great vocals, great songs, great ideas, but there was just this one ingredient missing, which was the Mick Ronson, the Keith Richards, the whatever you want to call it.'

Hut label manager Dave Boyd echoed the producer's thoughts.

'I think Richard realised in his heart that it couldn't be The Verve without Nick... What Nick does, even on stage, sounds like what you'd need three guitarists and a programmer to do.'

While turmoil continued to surround the band, Noel Gallagher, as if to mark the passing time and the gulf that had opened up between both bands, invited Ashcroft to perform a solo spot at their Madison Square Garden show in New York in March 1996. Ashcroft opened for Oasis by performing three acoustic numbers to a largely bemused American audience and realised then that he was a band member, nothing more or less.

As he told Dazed & Confused, 'That was mad, really; it just showed me that I'm not a solo artist. I felt so alone up there.'

Judging by his heartfelt reaction, it came as no surprise that the rumours that he would also perform solo at both the Oasis Knebworth and Loch Lomond shows would come to nothing.

Later in the year, in a move that seemed to question all reason, they returned to Wales – Rockfield Studios this time – to record with Owen Morris. The difficulties faced this time, though, were not to involve broken soundproof glass, Syd Barrett or MDMA on a scale that would make the most ardent clubber blanch. After two weeks spent trying to raise their new material to their own characteristically high standards, the sessions were brought to a halt. For reasons which were now making themselves achingly clear, it simply wasn't working.

Two things happened before Richard Ashcroft finally picked up the phone to call Nick McCabe asking him to rejoin the band. Firstly, Ashcroft's psychic advisor, a member of the spiritualist church near his home in west London, instructed

Ashcroft approached former Stone Roses guitarist John Squire... Ironically, at the time, it was rumoured that McCabe had been approached about becoming the new guitarist in the Stone Roses

Richard to recruit McCabe back in to the band. Secondly, the night before the phone call, Nick McCabe had a dream where he was once again working in a quantity surveyor's office in Liverpool. Work was enjoyable and satisfying; his work mates liked him, they made him tea. Before he woke, he says he remembers thinking that he had a purpose in life again, how happy it all made him. Then the phone rang.

It was January 1997, the pair hadn't spoken to each other for eighteen months. In reports of that initial call, McCabe has said that Ashcroft ate shit before he asked him back. Ashcroft will only admit to being humble. Their recollection of events might differ, but the outcome now seems gregarious and charmed. It's obvious that in their own way, each missed the other.

Ashcroft told Q, 'I called him because I admire him and I want him to be with us. I didn't expect him to drop everything and do it. I thought he might say no.'

McCabe says his initial reaction was to tell the singer to fuck off, that a year before he'd wanted to kill him, but it was obvious to him that he needed The Verve as much as they needed him. The Verve, he says without prompting, are his first love.

Ashcroft obviously feels the same way. Speaking to Dazed & Confused after news of the reconciliation he sounded relieved and in some way grateful for what had become a temporary break up of the band.

'That eighteen months or whatever it is, has given us the strength to last another ten years... I tell ya, it's been the longest fuckin' road I've ever been down. The thing is, I love Nick McCabe and I never want to be in a band if he's not playing the guitar. I hope he thinks the same way about me. We just needed the time to realise it... ' Ψ

Ashcroft approached former Suede guitarist Bernard Butler. Rehearsals, which began at Bernard's house and were rumoured to be going splendidly, peaked at around a week... The search, it's reasonable to assume, was still on

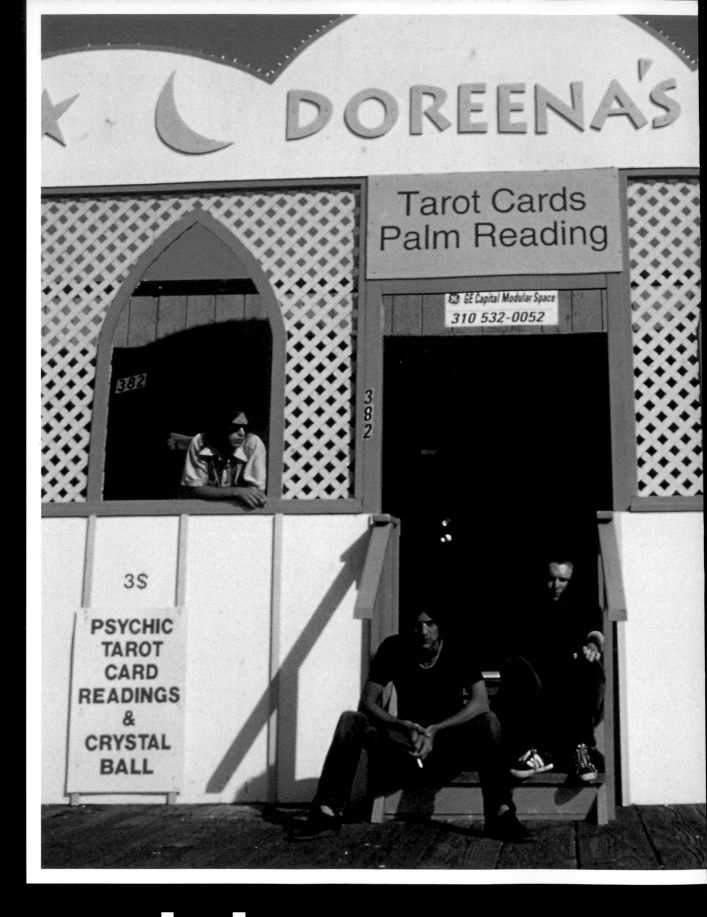

3$

DORINA'S
PALM
READINGS
&
TAROT
CARDS

s has given us the strength to

ast another **ten years**

The Verve, not unlike some of the musical legends whose greatness they aspire to, have left a trail of bad luck that, retrospectively, seems to have plagued their every step. Some of them call it the Verve Voodoo, others the Curse of The Verve, sometimes they won't talk about it at all.

Publicly, it first struck in 1994 when Verve were forced to prefix their name due to impending legal action from US jazz label, Verve. Things were beginning to move for the band both here and in the US, it seemed like the sensible thing to do. In the same year, just before the band were due to play their first Glastonbury Festival, drummer Peter Salisbury walked in to his kitchen to get a glass of water and somehow ended up shattering his foot to the point where he needed metal plates to repair the damage.

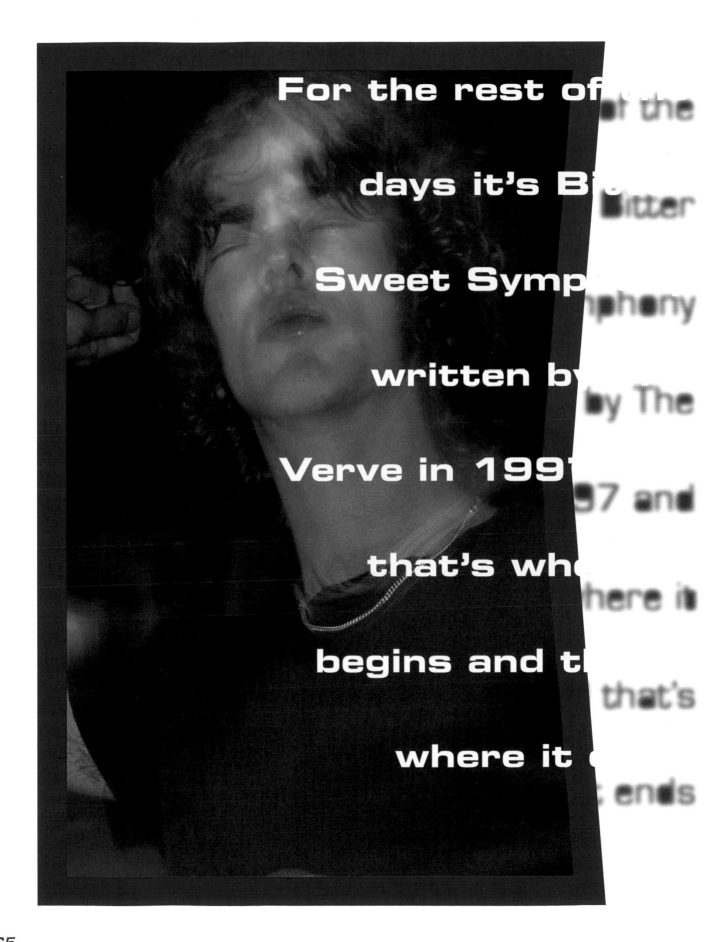

For the rest of the days it's Bitter Sweet Symphony written by The Verve in 1997 and that's where it begins and that's where it ends

Their first chance to achieve festival infamy was duly cancelled. As Ashcroft pointed out to Vox, 'A fuckin' kitchen. Only us! Would've been alright if there had been some incident.'

In Paris the following year, Nick McCabe was thrown down some stairs by a French security guard while attempting to get into his own dressing room. The fall broke his hand and the chance to support Oasis in Sheffield.

When they finally got onto the bill at Glastonbury, McCabe's amp blew up and, somehow, the TV feed came off-line for the entire duration of their set.

Their comeback tour, scheduled to begin in June 1997, was suddenly pulled when Ashcroft contracted a virus that caused his throat to swell and made singing, let alone performing, near impossible. As he's remarked since, he didn't want to wait this long just to go out and do the whole thing half-heartedly. So The Verve grumbled about the voodoo and waited.

Other instances of failure chasing their fame that have been cited by the band in articles can usually be traced back and blame placed on the band themselves. Ashcroft's collapse on the US tour was, by admission of the then band manager, John Best, pretty much a case of taking God-knows what and then forgetting the little things like drinking water and occasionally putting food in your mouth.

While stories of Radio One sessions cancelled at a day's notice because the band had spent the entire night swimming in a pool while tripping out of their heads, coming to poolside at seven in the morning, could hardly be the fault of dark forces or circumstance. At least they woke up.

As if there hadn't been enough cruel irony in The Verve's short career, it seems that their love of the Rolling Stones was the one thing that could possibly mar their resounding comeback. The band who often stumbled under the weight of Richards/Jagger comparisons, especially physically, were about to be knocked sideways simply by paying their respects.

By the time that Bitter Sweet Symphony was released on 16 June 1997, its familiar uplifting refrain of strings and plaintive solitude was already branded onto the national psyche. Radio One's Jo Whiley had already made it her record of the week five weeks before release. Mark Radcliffe did the

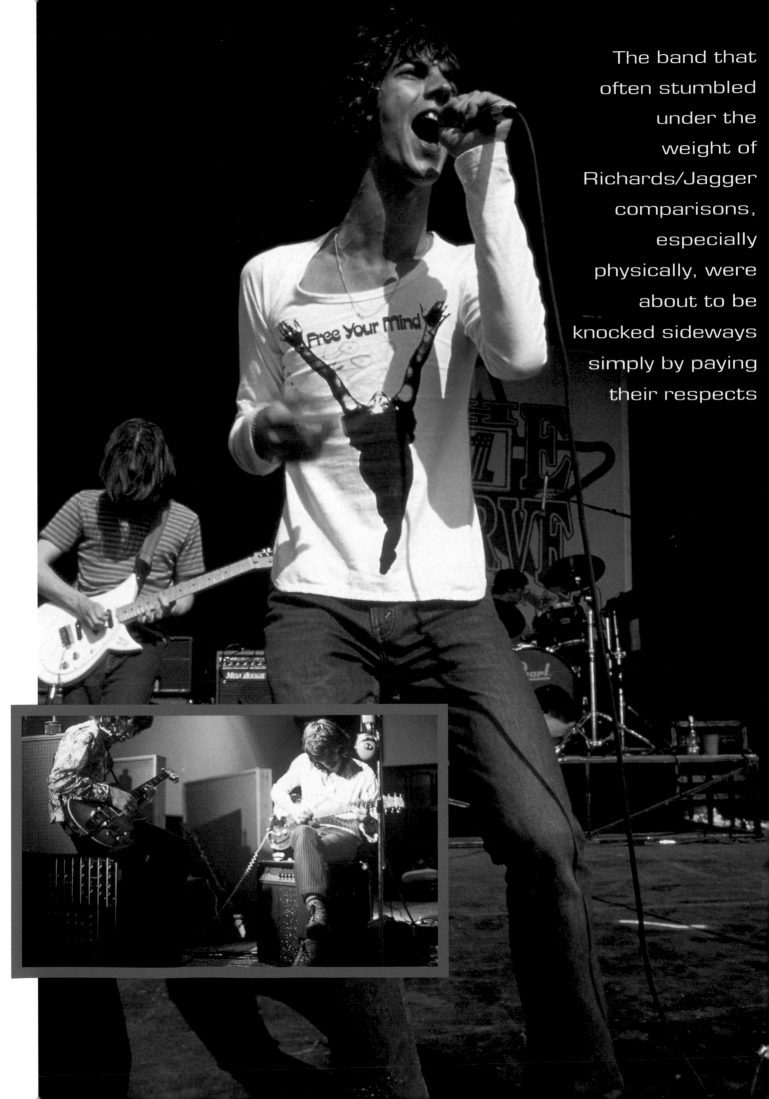

The band that often stumbled under the weight of Richards/Jagger comparisons, especially physically, were about to be knocked sideways simply by paying their respects

We are so much be

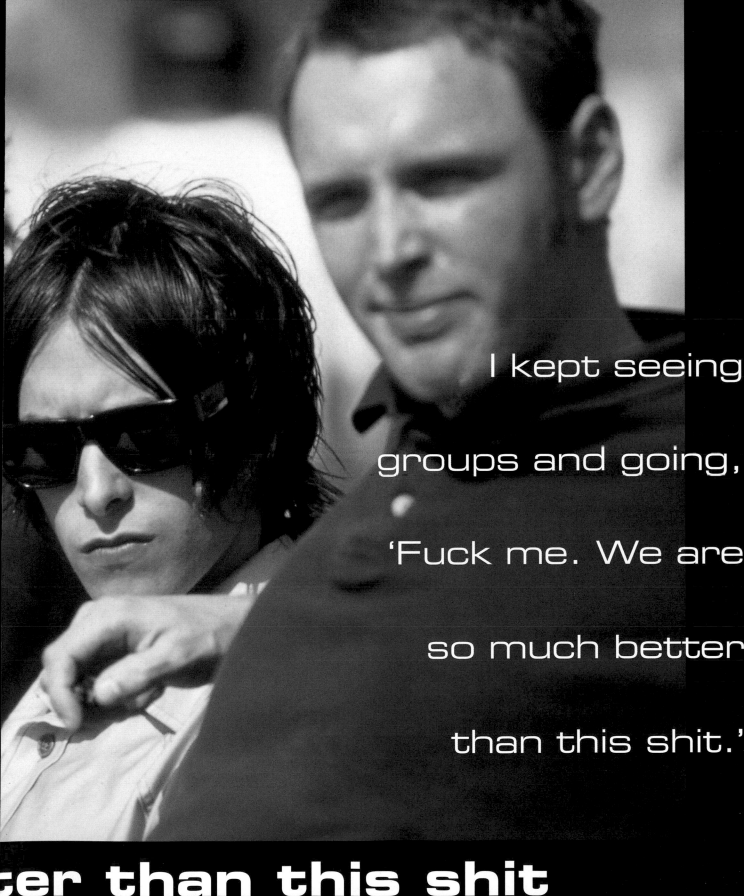

I kept seeing

groups and going,

'Fuck me. We are

so much better

than this shit.'

ter than this shit

same thing seven days later. NME were so taken with the entire thing that they put the band on the cover weeks before the single was due. The consensus was that something very special was about to happen; that a band who had promised so much before falling away, strangled artistically by their own hand, were now making good on a promise that had been sent out four years previously.

Hut manager David Boyd, an ardent supporter from day one, described them as a crucial English band. The Verve had somehow taken stock, Tong was kept on to supplement their sound with guitar and keyboards. While, in what was beginning to look not unlike a new dawn, they'd also changed management, opting to work with Big Life supremo, and former Wham! manager, Jazz Summers. The two had met through former Killing Joke bassist turned very successful producer Youth, who had helped work on the initial sessions for what was to be Urban Hymns. The band, possibly reflecting their new-found independence and evident strength, eventually elected to produce the body of the record themselves with help of engineer Chris Potter.

Youth, who Summers also manages, played him part of the sessions he'd worked on. His reaction to the result, as Summers told Music Week, was nothing short of wonder. 'I wasn't really a mad fan of theirs... But I remember hearing The Drugs Don't Work for the first time and just standing there with a big lump in my throat. Sometimes in this business, you can have shitty days... and sometimes you know why you're in the business.'

Ashcroft says he admires Summers because he's a maverick, much like The Verve, but it shouldn't be overlooked that Ashcroft was now savvy enough to realise that the band needed powerful representation in the US, a market where A Northern Soul had failed to live up to expectations. The Verve were looking to be an international band. Big Life could, it was argued, at least offer them the chance to show the world what they could do.

The unprecedented start to what promised to be the grandest of returns was still shrouded by shadows. Former

The band received a letter from Andrew Loog Oldham (above, left) approving of the song and the Stones were said to be pleased with how the song sounded

Beatles and Rolling Stones manager Allen Klein, who now administers the Stones' pre-1970 catalogue, claimed that the sample loop that the band had used for Bitter Sweet Symphony meant that the Stones were entitled to all royalties from the sale of the record. The familiar string leitmotif, the lyrics and the melody – essentially all you really remember from the song – are all the work of The Verve.

The original sample, a string and a bell loop, taken from Andrew Loog Oldham's orchestral arrangement of the Stones' The Last Time, comes from an entire album of classically-arranged Rolling Stones songs. Not only was the body of the royalties demanded, but a change to the album credits was levered into place. The sleeve now has the song credited to Jagger and Richards while Ashcroft gets a nod for his lyrics and vocals. The rest of the band don't even merit a mention. The music, according to the notes, comes courtesy of The Andrew Oldham Orchestra. The rumours that circulated before the album's release – that the single wouldn't make it onto the finished album – come as no

surprise considering the heartache and confusion it's since caused within the band.

Ashcroft, an ardent Stones fan, was very nearly inconsolable in interview. He spoke of taking a philosophical approach to the whole thing, of trying to see beyond it. The band received a letter from Andrew Loog Oldham approving of the song and the Stones were said to be pleased with how the song sounded but, when it came down to it, for Klein at least, it was another band working with the Stones' material for their own ends.

'We took a bit of bongos and a bit of strings… ' an exasperated Ashcroft told the NME. 'And we gave away probably one of the biggest worldwide hits of the fucking year… It's like when you hear those stories about Brian Wilson having his fucking tunes sold by his dad. It was one of them situations. Forever, no matter what happens… they fucking wrote that tune.

'It's horrible, it's a pisser and it's a downer, but it's beautiful. Because as the song says, "You're a slave to the money and then you die." I'll build and we'll make another

Former Beatles and Stones manager Allen Klein (above, left) decided that the Stones were entitled to all royalties from the sale of the record

fucking symphony. It makes me fucking want to puke when I think about it... but I also find it sadistically amazing because who gives a shit at the end of the day, because it's our song. For the rest of the days it's Bitter Sweet Symphony written by The Verve in 1997 and that's where it begins and that's where it ends.'

When Ashcroft spoke of a worldwide hit, it wasn't simply anger-fuelled rhetoric. The single was to chart not only at number two in the UK, but also reached that position in Italy and Saudi Arabia. It made waves all across Europe and went top ten in such unlikely places as Thailand and Turkey.

The video was as unforgettable as the song around which it was built. Filmed in the East End of London by director Walter Stern, who shot the Prodigy's Firestarter and Breathe promos, the premise is as unremitting a loop of images as the jangle of sounds travelling beneath it. Ashcroft glares ahead, walking along alone; upbeat in the face of adversity. Pushing against passers by, being attacked, though drawn inexorably on to his destination. He says he still gets people stopping their cars in the street to shout at him, to tell him to stop, that the video's over. There's no need to draw parallels or create a metaphor to measure up the struggles that he and the band have faced in order to reach their goals. There is both pain and ultimate celebration here. The actions match the simple purity of the lyrics, in which Ashcroft opens up distressingly. What is the more remarkable, is that between The Verve and Stern, they have created a video that is as beguiling as the song it serves to highlight and celebrate.

Tainted as the whole thing may have been, there was still simple pleasure to be gleaned from its success. Ashcroft discovered that Wigan had its first local radio station for years; Wish FM, playing classic hits. Enough people considered Bitter Sweet Symphony something of a classic for Ashcroft to call up the station and request the single for himself. To allay suspicions that it wasn't Ashcroft on the phone, but some hoaxer, he sang the song a cappella down the receiver to convince the station to plug the single. As he delighted in telling Vox, 'They put it straight on after Bon Jovi's You Give Love A Bad Name. Three cabbies sitting outside the station in Wigan going, "Er?".'

When the fuss concerning samples and royalty payments had finally died down, it became clear that all the talk of building another symphony to match the album's first brilliant single was neither an empty promise or a premise designed to hide their pain.

The Drugs Don't Work, their first number one single, had been written by Ashcroft some two years before. As he's reiterated in interviews, it's not so much a call to ease off on their indulgences, but a love letter sent out somewhere. Much like the regard given Ashcroft by Noel Gallagher (Cast No Shadow), succumbing to questions that attempted to peer too deeply into the heart of the singer, or song, were not encouraged.

'There's lines in there that are personal to me and personal to someone close to me and I can't really go into that side of things too much,' a reluctant Ashcroft told Vox. 'Most of us know what it feels like to be on the fucking floor and to love someone enough to know that if anything happened to them, you'd go in as well. The thought that your love is predestined and if one of you dies you're destined to meet again... I think everyone believes that when they're in love... it will go on forever and if anything ever happened I'm fucking with yer.'

As the band's reputation was beginning to blossom, the news that Ashcroft and Kate Radley from Spiritualized were now together was beginning to leak out to the press. The bands had first met as far back as 1992 when they'd toured together. When Ashcroft spoke of love, it seemed the stories could now be traced back to the source. It was clear that he hated the attention from the start. It wasn't what he or the band were about. Although A Northern Soul had cried out for some emotional stability, some loving sustenance, Urban Hymns would be a record that dealt in love, but found itself bound up with exploring the human condition; searching for the ambiguities and nuances of life. This record was not about Ashcroft dropping his guard or opening himself out. It was going to be bigger than that.

He responded to enquiries, discreet or otherwise, about his personal life with the memorable response that if people couldn't mind their own business then they'd be hit over the head with a baseball bat. Ashcroft would see to it, personally.

Years of promise, and fleeting highlights, only served to remind those listening that even though capable of greatness, The Verve were also the ones truly capable of destroying their own destiny. No one got in the way more than themselves. In the early autumn of 1997, after two remarkable singles, The Verve shrugged off any doubters and released an album that was perhaps as uncompromising as any of their previous work. It was so powerful that it made everything you might have heard up until then seem simply washed out and bleached of colour. Ashcroft's eager songwriting boasts to Q before the album's release were about to be realised. 'It's a gift; not something that's handed out free down the fucking shops. We have innate taste. No-one tells us what's shit and what's not. We know.'

The reports of Hut boss David Boyd being rendered speechless on first hearing tracks from the album weren't simple hype. Stories that everyone who had been in the studio during recording couldn't wait to ring their friends and tell them, suddenly didn't seem so stupid. It was an album you wanted to share, to help people discover. The Verve reference points were intact; the sprays of psychedelia, the sonic booms juxtaposed with penetrating silence. Ashcroft's imploring lilt and exuberant heckling all rounded off with words from within. It sounded like a record from another decade, another time. But then, perhaps that was the idea. It finally came to fruition at nine in the morning at Nomis Studios in west London. The Urban Hymns sessions were finally complete, fully formed.

Ashcroft, drawing on references from teenage years of eclectic record collecting, could barely contain his excitement when he spoke to Vox. 'You won't be disappointed. It's diverse, everything there, totally us. It's like a Roxy Music thing going on, we can do anything! Two of the biggest fuckin' massive slabs that we have ever done.'

Blundering rhetoric is doomed to pursue Urban Hymns as journalists, critics and pundits attempt to make sense of its divine voice. Rarely has the quintessence of life been so keenly sketched out; its lines are both clear and vibrant.

Ashcroft says the results of the record aren't happy coincidence or bewildering fate. The Verve had the blueprints drawn up a long time ago. As he would tell Dazed & Confused, between the release of the first two singles from the album, this record came from inside of themselves. 'It's just a question of putting the truth back into music... As we

News that Ashcroft and Kate Radley from Spiritualized were now together was beginning to leak out to the press

get nearer the end of the century people will demand to hear stuff that's from the fucking heart and nothing else will do. We've had a century where shit has been fed to us and, in the next century, people will realise that it's time for a fucking change. And the bigger The Verve get, the quicker it's gonna come... '

The cover shot of the band sitting together on a grassy bank was taken out behind their old school in Wigan, where teenagers would sneak out to have a smoke. McCabe's looking one way, the rest of the band, another. Though perhaps more tellingly, on the inner sleeve of the album, someone's let their black Labrador run loose over the band and all they can do is sprawl out and laugh. It looks a long way from the heavy glare of the four young men sat with the toy dolls on the A Storm In Heaven album. It almost looks like a different group of people altogether.

Ashcroft was heard to reflect on the emptiness of the two years spent trying to put things back together. Of

having the original dream and watching it disappear in the tumble of problems that had arisen within the band and within himself. Sometimes just wondering if he's done the right thing.

'I'm quite a mixed up person,' a genuinely perturbed Ashcroft would later tell Melody Maker. 'because you choose your road and you go down it and halfway down you maybe wish you'd just gone for the house and the job and lived the easy life, 'cos often you look around yourself and everyone else seems really happy. I remember going into the street where I live, while I was going through the madness of the last two years, and everyone's really happy in those picture and piano houses.'

But the rewards of making the right choice were to be beyond belief. The press fell over themselves, stumbling with sheer praise, admiration and awe. After the release of Oasis' rather pedestrian Be Here Now, it came as something of a relief to be able to wholeheartedly celebrate a British band not so caught up in themselves that they could only offer diminishing returns. It came as a shock, but not an unpleasant one.

Commercially, The Verve were now a real force. A number one single, and a number one album from the most unlikely of places. Ashcroft didn't pretend to understand or really welcome the commercial success. When the first single had raced up the charts to a number two spot and sat there for weeks, he'd been reluctant to celebrate their mass appeal. It wasn't why they were here.

He explained his reservations to The Face. 'The idea of Bitter Sweet Symphony being number two scares me a bit. I don't want loads of little kids listening to our tracks. It's not right. There is a loss of innocence in our music that I don't want them to hear.'

Reservations or not, the album was to touch people on a grand scale. In its first week it sold more than a quarter of a million copies in the UK. Comparatively, for sheer speed of sales, it was up there with bands like U2 and The Prodigy. It shifted 1.5 million copies worldwide in under two weeks. The string of British dates pencilled in for the beginning of 1998 sold out in two hours. The Verve were themselves responsible for a host of silly statistics and figures, all of them good. Suddenly losing all that money and creative credit to Allen Klein didn't cast such a damning shadow.

The series of sell-out shows supporting Oasis at Earl's Court only stood to reconfirm their new-found status. The reviews were ecstatic for a band who had almost always insisted that they were a very viable proposition live.

As Ashcroft, thwarted by the lay-off from live work that had been imposed upon them during the McCabe hiatus, had told Q magazine before a show at Manchester Academy, 'I'm in the greatest fuckin' band in the fuckin' world and I haven't been having it live for eighteen months, which has been a massive frustration. I kept seeing groups and going, "Fuck me. We are so much better than this shit." I was embarrassed for all of them.

'(With us) it's all about raising standards, raising the fucking levels of consciousness... When I saw the Roses all them years ago, it was inspiring... They showed me that there was another world, way beyond mediocrity. That's where The Verve have always aspired to being.'

In interview Ashcroft still speaks of higher things, of reaching beyond himself to convey understanding. In the not-so-distant past the press were quick to label his idiosyncrasies as the work of a madman. On their 1997 album, he finishes off the record in Come On by calling up God from a phonebox. Disturbingly, the emotion he conveys in his words makes the whole thing sound remarkably plausible.

As one journalist pointed out to him, as the album spiralled brilliantly upward, no one called him mad anymore. 'I know,' observed a cool Ashcroft. 'It seems I've been cured.'

It may be too close now, but the observation that Urban Hymns will stand to say something well in to the next millennium doesn't seem beyond reason.

All the talk towards the end of the vacuous 1980s, a decade Ashcroft loathes with a passion, were of the 1990s; that the future would be our redemption. Our self-serving ethos crafted in twelve turbulent years of Thatcherism, based on an ideal of free enterprise and profit-mongering, could be wiped away if only we could cleanse ourselves in the approaching ten years. But the 1990s, a decade that was meant to level assumptions and purge us of our sins, rolled on in with indifferent equanimity.

Music, especially, continued to look over its shoulder, not content with knowing what the other guy was doing, but

The idea of Bitter Sweet Symphony being number two scares me a bit. I don't want loads of little kids listening to our tracks. It's not right

what the other guy had done. Governments changed, but nothing really changed. Music changed, but nothing really changed. People changed – but what changed? There wasn't a bright new tomorrow opening up. Suddenly, it wasn't about introspection or demystifying the self, it was about changing titles and tags, but not the thing that was living or breathing beneath it. It was a veil that The Verve were determined to look beyond.

Admittedly, there's no real case to be argued for The Verve being the band who have taken on the mantle of reshaping the sound and vision of music; it simply hasn't happened. Look carefully into Urban Hymns and you'll see Led Zeppelin, possibly something you might mistake for The Doors. But what, to an extent, is evident and has been lacking elsewhere in music for some time, is their obvious passion for what they're doing. The self-belief that wasn't ultimately babble was suddenly profound when connected to their songs. Theirs is a record as heartfelt and memorable as first love.

As Ashcroft had told Melody Maker while attempting to translate his feelings of the moment inspiration had touched him: 'I put out my antennae and I pull the music in. Keith Richards said a similar thing and, you see, Richards is so anti-bullshit, but even he has to recognise something beyond himself and a piece of wood. There's something else involved in the beginning of Gimme Shelter, it's magic, it's pure. All I can see is that all inspiration is out there, every past, present and future, every note. Handel's Messiah came to him in a flash... As far as true inspiration's concerned, it's all out there for the taking. It's about rejecting the conditioning... and just opening up to it, just... receiving.'

Urban Hymns looked up and held its arms open wide. As an album, the initial reaction was how could they possibly follow this? The grace instilled in the record follows The Verve's familiar pattern of stealth and bombast. But whereas A Storm In Heaven ran in undistilled circles of sound and A Northern Soul came as a cry for help, for understanding, the grooves of this album are filled with hope. Not blind faith in the unknown, but conviction that better things can happen and they might just happen here.

Ashcroft's conviction that songwriting can be a powerful tool is strongly attested here. The message is never more

clear on songs such as the luxuriant Sonnet. A simplistic offer of love to someone built on a tide of strings. Its poignancy brought to bear by simple means.

The Rolling People retraces the familiar band swagger. After the understated start to the album, its dramatic punch is suddenly giddying and fresh, while Catching The Butterfly draws on McCabe's juddering guitar refrain that spreads out to break the boundaries of the song.

Ashcroft explained it to Melody Maker: 'We were always into that Can method of cutting up tapes. The first time we played the song Nick came up with an amazing effect on his guitar and we just built it from there... We sometimes get into this frame of mind that we can't beat machines where grooves are concerned, and it's bollocks.'

The sparse Neon Wilderness would be the last thing to be finished on the album. Coming to at around seven in the morning, it reflects the despondency and listlessness of bar-hopping alone in the early hours. Ashcroft says he can imagine it playing somewhere behind Midnight Cowboy.

It's said the melancholy yet uplifting Space And Time, written in the Spring of 1996, was such an inspiration to Liam Gallagher, that when Ashcroft played with Oasis in New York, Liam insisted that they get a cab back to the hotel so that he could hear the irresistible demo of the song one more time.

Weeping Willow works in a similar vein. Ashcroft says it's a more personal song, more to do with himself, his partner, the way she makes him look at life. Consequently, he's much more reluctant to discuss the lyrics, dismissing them out of hand as songwriter fodder. The music, however, delighted him beyond all comprehension. Again, talking to Melody Maker, he said, 'The guitars are like fucking Neil Young riding in hell. It's an amazing guitar sound in that bit, and some lovely touches of drumming. I'm just generally positive about that song... '

Ashcroft sounded both upbeat and generous. An age away from the disillusioned singer who had temporarily thrown away his dreams, after the T In The Park show, breaking the back of the band before fleeing to Cornwall and self-imposed solitude.

His new-found optimism even echoed through in the title of what was to be their third single, Lucky Man. In conversation, he's admitted its upbeat premise; that there are good things to be found and embraced in life.

One Day pored over the remains of childhood, looking inward and trying to rediscover the simple joys of being a child. It spoke of seeing beyond the now, being strong enough mentally and spiritually to face whatever it is that's coming.

It's odd to consider that Ashcroft will write a song of love and dismiss it out of hand when questioned closely about it, but is more than willing to leave himself open to possible ridicule with regard to the philosophies, inspirations and beliefs spelt out within his music. It's one of the things that helps to set him apart as a lyricist and songwriter.

This Time came to life with the help of a handful of metal coat hangers. The rippling sheen of sound underneath the song is a set of them recorded, slowed down and washed with effects. The result is surprising. One is rarely truly

It's a gift; not something that's handed out free down the fucking shops

When I saw the Roses all them years ago, it was inspiring... They showed me that there was another world, way beyond mediocrity. That's where The Verve have always aspired to being

moved by a household object. Lyrically, Ashcroft looks to himself within the song. He says the song speaks for him, about him. He admits to his weaknesses, to his failings as a human being and how he's constantly attempting to redefine himself as a person.

'When I sing, "I'm gonna rise into the light" on that, for me it means I can get better without any base religion or a strict philosophy on life,' he told Melody Maker. 'There's millions of us out there who haven't got that and are actually hurtling through life trying to get little pieces from different sources to try and find our own inner philosophies and our inner strength from something else.'

The halcyon Velvet Morning, with its waves of dissonance built around the uneasy mantra of 'Life is a game you try', is the song that alone could elevate them to legendary status. It's something that a song as able and genuine as this one doesn't instantly shape the album itself. It simply becomes a distinguished peer among very good company indeed.

Ashcroft understands the weight of his work, but now assured within himself, isn't without humour about the whole thing.

'It's touching on those moments at seven or eight in the morning when you've gone from thinking you've solved the fucking world's problems to feeling like shit and walk out for a pint of milk...' he told Melody Maker. 'It was another great night with the orchestra, and that loudhailer I'm singing through I just bought from a car boot sale the week before recording it. I just did it on the spot, but if you speed it up it sounds like a classic country hit!'

The album finally topples over sideways with the exuberant Come On. A boisterous blow out that culminates in something that sounds not unlike MC5 and Led Zeppelin hanging one on. Ashcroft is pinned somewhere in the middle of the mix, his voice passing in and out of the speakers as if he's standing on the wrong side of the studio. His cries of 'Fuck you' are both deranged and delighted. It's not the roar of a man bloodied by life, but one with his head up, arms held high. A rallying call to those who want to hear it.

As he told Melody Maker, 'That is the "fuck you" of a man who's on top of it, who's buzzing, who's got those guitars raging underneath him. It's a "fuck you" of total joy.'

The album finally settles into silence as the onslaught fades. The only sound reaching up out of the calm darkness is that of McCabe's guitar, lifting gently as a baby's cry is heard buoyed by the sound.

The Verve are already looking ahead. The boasts of their becoming the new Led Zeppelin are not without merit. Remember how everyone chuckled when Ashcroft insisted that one day, in around three albums time, they'd have the avid attention of a world eager to listen? He said they'd be very important, whether that was reflected in their sales or not. There's a purity in their convictions that's almost religious and you can't help but be drawn in.

They've already made an application to the Ministry of Defence for permission to use old defence sites, abandoned airfields and dry docks, to stage huge event shows, showcasing their talents as something more than simply another band.

Ashcroft reasoned to Q, 'I think we've got that power in our sound to fill a huge space and to still connect with people.'

You can see him now: Ashcroft standing out there at the edge of things, laying demons to rest, hands held upward to the night sky. Peering into the distance, still searching upward, drawing dreams down while reaching for those most elusive of stars. ⓦ

**I put out my antennae and I pull
the music in**

Discography

Single releases

9 March 1992 – All In The Mind
Tracks: All In The Mind, One Way To Go, Man Called Sun
Label: Hut Recordings
Formats:
UK Cat #: HUTT12: 12" Single released 09/03/92
UK Cat #: HUT12: 7" Single released 09/03/92 – deleted 04/07/94
UK Cat #: HUTCD12: CD Single released 09/03/92

22 June 1992 – She's A Superstar
Tracks: She's A Superstar, Feel
Label: Hut Recordings
Formats:
UK Cat #: HUTCD16: CD Single released 22/06/92
UK Cat #: HUT16: 7" Single released 22/06/92 – deleted 18/04/94
UK Cat #: HUTT16: 12" Single released 22/06/92

5 October 1992 – Gravity Grave
Tracks: Gravity Grave (Extended Version), Endless Life, Man Called Sun (Live), Gravity Grave (Live Encore)
Label: Hut Recordings.
UK Chart: 196
Formats:
UK Cat #: HUTCD21: CD Single released 05/10/92
UK Cat #: HUTT21: 12" Single released 05/10/92
UK Cat #: HUTEN21: 10" Single released 05/10/92 – deleted 04/07/94

10 May 1993 – Blue
Tracks: Blue, Twilight, Where The Geese Go, No Come Down
UK Chart: 69
Formats:
UK Cat #: HUTT29: 12" Single released 10/05/93
UK Cat #: HUTEN29: 10" Single released 10/05/93 – deleted 04/07/94
UK Cat #: HUTCD29: CD Single released 10/05/93

1 June 1993 – Make It 'Til Monday
Tracks: Make It 'Til Monday (Live Glastonbury '93)
Label: Hut Recordings
Formats: UK Cat #: FLEXY1: Flexidisc (promo) – deleted

20 September 1993 – Slide Away
Tracks: Slide Away, Make It 'Til Monday (Acoustic), Virtual World (Acoustic), 6 O'clock
Label: Hut Recordings
UK Chart: 98
Formats:
UK Cat #: HUTT35: 12" Single released 20/09/93
UK Cat #: HUTCD35: CD Single released 20/09/93
UK Cat #: HUT35: 7" Single released 20/09/93 – deleted 04/07/94

1 May 1995 – This Is Music
Tracks: This Is Music, Let The Damage Begin, You And Me
Label: Hut Recordings
UK Chart: 35
Formats:
UK Cat #: HUTT54: 12" Single released 01/05/95
UK Cat #: HUTCD54: CD Single released 01/05/95
UK Cat #: HUT54: 7" Single released 01/05/95
Non UK Cat #: HUTDE54: CD Single released 01/05/95

12 June 1995 – On Your Own
Tracks: On Your Own, I See The Door, Little Gem, Dance On Your Bones
Label: Hut Recordings
UK Chart:28
Formats: UK Cat #: HUT55: 7" Single released 12/06/95
UK Cat #: HUTC55: Cassette Single released 12/06/95 – deleted 21/06/96
UK Cat #: HUTCD55: CD Single released 12/06/95

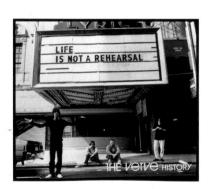

18 September 1995 – History
Tracks: History (Radio Edit), Back On My Feet Again, On Your Own (Acoustic), Monkey Magic (Brainstorm Mix), History, Grey Skies, Life's Not A Rehearsal
Label: Hut Recordings
UK Chart: 24
Formats:
UK Cat #: HUTCD59: CD Single released 18/09/95
UK Cat #: HUTC59: Cassette Single released 18/09/95 – deleted 21/06/96
Non UK Cat #: HUTDE59 CD Single released 18/09/95
UK Cat #: HUTDX59: CD Single released 18/09/95
UK Cat #: HUTCDP59: CD Single (promo) – deleted
UK Cat #: HUTCDP59: CD Single (promo) – deleted

2 June 1997 – Bitter Sweet Symphony 12" promo
Tracks: Bitter Sweet Symphony (Alt Version), Bitter Sweet
Symphony (MSG mix)
Label: Hut Recordings
Formats: UK Cat #: HUTTP82: 12" Single (promo) released
02/06/97 (not available to public)

16 June 1997 – Bitter Sweet Symphony
Tracks: Bitter Sweet Symphony, Lord I Guess I'll Never Know,
Country Song, Bitter Sweet Symphony (Radio Edit), Bitter
Sweet Symphony (Extended Version), So Sister, Echo Bass
Label: Hut Recordings
UK Chart: 2
Formats:
UK Cat #: HUTDG82: CD Single released 16/06/97
UK Cat #: HUTC82: Cassette Single released 16/06/97
UK Cat #: HUTDX82: CD Single released 16/06/97
Non UK Cat #: 8943752: CD Single released 16/06/97
Non UK Cat #: HUTCDE82: CD Single released 16/06/97
UK Cat #: HUTTR82: 12" Single (promo) (not available to
public)
UK Cat #: HUTCDP82: CD Single (promo) (not available to
public)
UK Cat #: HUTTP82: 12" Single (promo) (not available to
public)
Non UK Cat #: 8943606: 12" Single released 16/06/97

**28 July 1997 – Bitter Sweet Symphony (James
Lavelle Remix)**
Tracks: Bitter Sweet Symphony (James Lavelle Instrumental
Remix), Bitter Sweet Symphony (James Lavelle Remix)
Label: Hut Recordings.
Formats:
UK Cat #: HUTTR82: 12" Single (promo) released
28/07/97 (not available to public)

1 September 1997 – The Drugs Don't Work
Tracks: The Drugs Don't Work (Full Length), Bitter Sweet
Symphony (James Lavelle Remix), The Crab, Stamped, The
Drugs Don't Work (Radio Edit), Three Steps, The Drugs Don't
Work (Original Demo)
Label: Hut Recordings
UK Chart: 1
Formats:
UK Cat #: HUTC88: Cassette Single released 01/09/97
UK Cat #: HUTDG88: CD Single released 01/09/97

Non UK Cat #: HUTCD88: CD Single released 01/09/97
UK Cat #: HUTDX88: CD Single released 01/09/97
UK Cat #: HUTCDP88: CD Single (promo) (not available to public)
Non UK Cat #: HUTCDJ88: CD Single (promo) (not available to public)

24 November 1997 – Lucky Man

Tracks: Lucky Man, Never Wanna See You Cry, History, MSG, The Longest Day, Lucky Man (Happiness More Or Less)
Label: Hut Recordings
Formats:
UK Cat #: HUTDX 92: CD single 1 released 24/11/97
UK Cat #: HUTDG 92: CD single 2 released 24/11/97
UK Cat #: HUTC 92: Audio Cassette released 24/11/97

EP releases

7 December 1992 – The Verve EP

Tracks: Gravity Grave (Edit), Man Called Sun, She's A Superstar (Edit), Endless Life, Feel
Label: Hut Recordings.
Formats:
UK Cat #: HUTUS1: CD Album released 07/12/92

Album releases

1 March 1993 – Voyager 1 (US)

Tracks: Slide Away, Gravity Grave, One Way To Go, South Pacific, Already There, She's A Superstar
Bootleg album release. Recorded live in London and New York 1992, 1000 copies pressed on blue vinyl, 300 of which were ruined en route to the USA

21 June 1993 – A Storm In Heaven

Tracks: Star Sail, Slide Away, Already There, Beautiful Mind, The Sun The Sea, Virtual World, Make It 'Til Monday, Blue, Butterfly, See You In The Next One (Have A Good Time)
Label: Hut Recordings
UK Chart: 27
Formats:
UK Cat #: HUTLP10: 12" LP released 21/06/93
UK Cat #: HUTMC10: Single Play Cassette released 21/06/93
UK Cat #: CDHUT10: CD Album released 21/06/93

23 May 1994 – No Come Down

Tracks: No Come Down, Blue (USA Mix), Make It 'Til Monday (Acoustic), Butterfly (Acoustic), Where The Geese Go, 6 O'clock, One Way To Go, Gravity Grave (Live Glastonbury 93), Twilight (appeared on USA version only)
Label: Vernon Yard/Hut Recordings
Formats: UK Cat #:CDHUT18: CD Album released 17/05/94

3 July 1995 – A Northern Soul

Tracks: A New Decade, This Is Music, On Your Own, So It Goes, A Northern Soul, Brainstorm Interlude, Drive You Home, History, No Knock On My Door, Life's An Ocean, Stormy Clouds, Stormy Clouds (Reprise)
Label: Hut Recordings
UK Chart: 13
Formats:
UK Cat #: HUTLP27: 2 x 12" LPs released 03/07/95
UK Cat #: HUTMC27: Single Play Cassette released 03/07/95
UK Cat #: CDHUT27: CD Album released 03/07/95
UK Cat #: DGHUT27: CD Album released 03/07/95 – deleted 04/07/96

29 September 1997 – Urban Hymns

Tracks: Bitter Sweet Symphony, Sonnet, The Rolling People, The Drugs Don't Work, Catching The Butterfly, Neon Wilderness, Space And Time, Weeping Willow, Lucky Man, One Day, This Time, Velvet Morning, Come On
Label: Hut Recordings
UK Chart: 1
Formats: UK Cat #: CDPHUT45: CD Album (promo)
UK Cat #: CDHUT45: CD Album released 29/09/97
UK Cat #: HUTMC45: Single Play Cassette released 29/09/97
UK Cat #: HUTLP45: 2 x 12" LPs released 29/09/97
UK Cat #: HUTLPX45: 2 x 12" LPs released 29/09/97

Pictures

The author and publishers have made every reasonable effort to contact all copyright holders. Any errors that may have occurred are inadvertent and anyone who for any reason has not been contacted is invited to write to the publishers so that a full acknowledgement may be made in subsequent editions of this work.